MW01670620

Warren Buffett

The Oracle of Omaha

Filiquarian Publishing, LLC.

Warren Buffett - The Oracle of Omaha is available for free download at www.biographiq.com/bookd/WB696

Filiquarian Publishing, LLC.

Warren Buffett

The Oracle of Omaha

Warren Edward Buffett (born August 30, 1930, Omaha, Nebraska) is an American investor, businessperson and philanthropist.

Often called the "Sage of Omaha" or the "Oracle of Omaha"[2], Buffett is currently the largest shareholder and CEO of Berkshire Hathaway. With an estimated current net worth of around US$56.9 billion,[1] he was ranked by Forbes as the third-richest person in the world as of April 11, 2007, behind Carlos Slim Helú and Bill Gates.[3]

Buffett is known for his unconventional style and frugality despite his immense wealth.[4] His 2006 annual salary of about $100,000[5] is tiny by the standards of senior executive remuneration in other comparable companies,[6] and when he spent $9.7 million of Berkshire's funds on a corporate jet in 1989, he jokingly named it "The Indefensible" because of his past criticisms of such purchases by other CEOs.[7] He continues to live in the same house in the central Dundee neighborhood of Omaha, Nebraska that he bought in 1958 for $31,500[8], today valued at around $700,000.[9]

Buffett is also a noted philanthropist. In 2006, he announced a plan to give away his fortune to charity, with 83% of it going to the Bill and Melinda Gates Foundation.[10] The donation will amount to approximately US$30 billion, at the time of the announcement enough to more than double the size of the foundation. In 2007, Buffett was listed among Time's 100 Most Influential People in The World.

Overview

Warren Buffett was born in Omaha, Nebraska to Howard Buffett, a stock broker and United States Representative, and his wife Leila Buffett. Warren Buffett displayed an extremely keen understanding of business and mathematics at a young age, easily doing complex mathematical computations in his head. He was also known as a bookworm who displayed an insatiable hunger for knowledge pertaining to business and capital markets. He began working at his father's brokerage at the age of 11, and that same year made his first stock purchase, buying Cities Services shares for $38.25 each. He sold them when the price reached $40, only to see them rocket to $200 a few years later.[11] This taught him the importance of investing in good companies for the long term. At the age of 14, he and a fellow high school student began installing pinball machines in barber shops. There have been rumors that Warren was in a band during this time, but that is not true. When recently asked if he plays any instruments, he stated that in the past he has played the ukulele and the trumpet.

Although he excelled as a student, he felt college would be a waste given his success as an entrepreneur. He already had money coming in from a number of newspaper routes he ran, as well as from Wilson Coin Op, a pinball machine company he had started with a friend, and from the passive income streams coming from a farmer paying rent to him for the use of his farm. He had saved $5,000 and graduated near the top 20 in his class at the age of16. He eventually yielded to his father's advice and decided to attend college.

Following his graduation from Washington, DC's Woodrow Wilson High School in 1947, Warren attended the Wharton School at the University of Pennsylvania for two years, then transferred to the University of Nebraska. There he began his interest in investing after reading Benjamin Graham's The Intelligent Investor.

He obtained a Master's degree in economics in 1951 at Columbia University, studying under Benjamin Graham, alongside other future value investors including Walter Schloss and Irving Kahn. Another influence on Buffett's investment philosophy was the well-known investor and writer Philip Fisher who wrote the book Common Stocks, Uncommon Profits. After receiving the only A+ Benjamin Graham ever handed out to a student in his security analysis class, Buffett wanted to work at Graham-Newman but was initially turned down. Instead, he went to work at his father's brokerage as a salesman until Graham offered him a position in 1954. Buffett returned to Omaha two years later, when Graham retired.

Buffett established Buffett Associates, Ltd., his first investment partnership, in 1956. It was financed by $100 from Buffett, the general partner, and $105,000 from seven limited partners consisting of Buffett's family and friends.[12]

Buffett created several additional partnerships which were later consolidated as Buffett Partnership Limited. He ran the partnerships out of his bedroom, adhering closely to Graham's investment approach and compensation structure. These investments made in excess of 30% compounded annually between 1956 to 1969, in a market where 7% to 11% was thc norm.

Buffett employed a three-pronged approach:

1. Generals: undervalued securities that possess margin of safety and meet expected return-to-risk characteristics[2]

2. Arbitrages: company events that are not related to broader market changes, such as mergers and acquisitions, liquidation, etc.

3. Controls: build sizable holdings, ally with other shareholders or employ proxies to effect changes in companies

In 1962 Buffett Partnerships began purchasing shares of Berkshire Hathaway, a large manufacturing company in the declining textile industry that was selling for less than its working capital. In 1969, Buffett would dissolve all his partnerships to focus on running Berkshire Hathaway. At the time, Charlie Munger, Berkshire's current Vice Chairman, remarked that purchasing the company was a mistake, due to the failure of the textile industry. Berkshire, however, became one of the largest holding companies in the world, as Buffett redirected the company's excess cash to acquire private businesses and stocks of public companies. At the core of his strategy were insurance companies, due to the large cash reserves they must keep on hand to pay out future claims. Essentially, the insurer does not own the reserve, but may invest it and keep any proceeds.

Under Munger's influence, Buffett's investment approach moved away from a strict adherence to Graham's principles, and he began to focus on high-quality businesses with enduring competitive advantages. Buffett described such advantages as an economic "moat"[3] that kept rivals at a safe distance, as opposed to commodity businesses, which sell undifferentiated products and face direct competition. A classic example of a wide-moat company is Coca-Cola, because consumers are willing to pay more for a Coke than for a generic beverage with a similar taste. On the other hand, salt is considered a commodity product because consumers generally have no preferences for one brand of salt over another.

Investment in wide-moat businesses has become a hallmark of Berkshire Hathaway, particularly when buying whole companies rather than public stocks. As a result, it now owns a large number of businesses which are dominant players in their respective industries, specialize in various niche markets, or possess other unique characteristics to separate them from their competitors.

Management Style

Warren Buffett views himself as a capital allocator above anything else. His primary responsibility is to allocate capital to businesses with good economics and keep their existing management to lead the company.

When Buffett acquires a controlling interest in a business, he makes clear to the owner the following:

* He will not interfere with the running of the company.

* He will be responsible for hiring and setting the compensation of the top executive.

* Capital allocated to the business will have a price tag (a hurdle rate) attached, usually a requirement of a return on capital in excess of fifteen percent. This process is to motivate owners to send excess capital that does not return more

than its cost to Berkshire headquarters rather than investing it at low returns. This cash is then free to be invested in opportunities that offer higher returns.

Buffett's hands-off approach has held strong appeal and created room for his managers to perform as owners and ultimate decision makers of their businesses. This acquisition strategy enabled Buffett to buy companies at fair prices because the sellers wanted room to operate independently after selling.

Besides his skills in managing Berkshire's cash flow, Buffett is skilled in managing the company's balance sheet. Since taking over Berkshire Hathaway, Buffett has weighed every decision against its impact on the balance sheet. As of 2005, he has succeeded in building Berkshire into one of the nine companies that are still rated by S&P as AAA, the highest credit rating achievable and thus, with the lowest cost of debt. Buffett takes comfort in his belief that, for the near future, his company will not be one of those shaken by economic or natural catastrophes. He has repeated over the years that his catastrophe insurance operation is the only one he knows of that can keep the checks clearing during a financial turmoil.

Investment Approach

Buffett's philosophy on business investing is a modification of the value investing approach of his mentor Benjamin Graham. Graham bought companies because they were cheap compared to their intrinsic value. He was of the belief that as long as the market undervalued them relative to their intrinsic value he was making a solid investment. He reasoned that the market will eventually realize it has undervalued the company and will correct its course regardless of what type of business the company was in. In addition he believed that the business has to have solid economics behind it. Buffett's investment style is also heavily influenced by Phil Fisher.

The following are some questions to determine what business to buy, based on the book Buffettology by Mary Buffett:

* Is the company in an industry with good economics, i.e., not an industry competing on price. Does the company have a consumer monopoly or brand name that commands loyalty? Can any company with an abundance of resources compete successfully with the company?

* Are the Owner Earnings on an upward trend with good and consistent margins?

* Is the debt-to-equity ratio low or is the earnings-to-debt ratio high, i.e. can the company repay debt even in years when earnings are lower than average?

* Does the company have high and consistent Returns on Invested Capital?

* Does the company retain earnings for growth?

* The business should not have high maintenance cost of operations, high capital expenditure or investment cash outflow. This is not the same as investing to expand capacity.

* Does the company reinvest earnings in good business opportunities? Does management have a good track record of profiting from these investments?

* Is the company free to adjust prices for inflation?

Buffett also concentrates when to buy. He does not want to invest in businesses with indiscernible value. He will wait for market corrections or downturns to buy solid businesses at reasonable prices, since stock market downturns present buying opportunities.

He is known for being conservative when speculation is rampant in the market and being aggressive when others are fearing for their capital. This contrarian strategy is what led Buffett's company through the Internet boom and bust without significant damage, although critics have also noted that it may have led Berkshire to miss out on potential opportunities during the same period.

He also asks at what price is the business a bargain, and his answer typically is when it provides a higher rate of compounded return relative to other available investment opportunities.

Warren Buffett's letters to shareholders are a valuable source in understanding his investment style and outlook.[13]

Philanthropy

In June 2006, Warren Buffett gave approximately 10 million Berkshire Hathaway Class B shares to the Bill & Melinda Gates Foundation (worth approximately USD 30.7 billion as of June 23 2006; see [4]) making it the largest charitable donation in history. The foundation will receive 5% of the total donation on an annualized basis each July, beginning in 2006. Buffett will also join the board of directors of the Gates Foundation, although he does not plan to be actively involved in running the foundation.

Buffett also announced plans to contribute additional Berkshire stock valued at approximately $6.7 billion to the Susan Thompson Buffett Foundation and to other foundations headed by his three children. This is a significant shift from previous statements Buffett has made, having stated that most of his fortune would pass to his Buffett Foundation. The bulk of the estate of his wife, valued at $2.6 billion, went to that foundation when she died in 2004.[5]

His children will not inherit a significant proportion of his wealth. These actions are consistent with statements he has made in the past indicating his opposition to the transfer of great fortunes from one generation to the next. Buffett once commented, "I want to give my kids just enough so that they would feel that they could do anything, but not so much that they would feel like doing nothing"[6].

The following two quotations from 1995 and 1988, respectively, highlight Warren Buffett's thoughts on his wealth and why he long planned to reallocate it:

"I personally think that society is responsible for a very significant percentage of what I've earned. If you stick me down in the middle of Bangladesh or Peru or someplace, you find out how much this talent is going to produce in the wrong kind of soil... I work in a market system that happens to reward what I do very well—disproportionately well. Mike Tyson, too. If you can knock a guy out in 10 seconds and earn $10 million for it, this world will pay a lot for that. If you can bat .360, this world will pay a lot for that. If you're a marvelous teacher, this world won't pay a lot for it. If you are a terrific nurse, this world will not pay a lot for it. Now, am I going to try to come up with some comparable worth system that somehow (re)distributes that? No, I don't think you can do that. But I do think that when you're treated enormously well by this market system, where in effect the market system showers the ability to buy goods and services on you because of some peculiar talent—maybe your adenoids are a certain way, so you can sing and everybody will pay you enormous sums to be on television or whatever—I think society has a big claim on that." (Lowe 1997:164–165)

"I don't have a problem with guilt about money. The way I see it is that my money represents an enormous number of claim checks on society. It's like I have these little pieces of paper that I can turn into consumption. If I wanted to, I could hire 10,000 people to do nothing but paint my picture every day for the rest of my life. And the GNP would go up. But the utility of the product would be zilch, and I would be keeping those 10,000 people from doing AIDS research, or teaching, or nursing. I don't do that though. I don't use very many of those claim checks. There's nothing material I want very much. And I'm going to give virtually all of those claim checks to charity when my wife and I die." (Lowe 1997:165–166)

Since 2000, Buffett has raised money for the Glide Foundation through online auctions. Bidders have donated up to $650,100 for the chance to have one meal with him.

In September 2006, Buffett auctioned his Lincoln Town Car to support Girls, Inc.[7] The vehicle sold for $73,200 on eBay.[8]

Writings

Warren Buffett's writings include his annual reports and various articles. In his article The Superinvestors of Graham-and-Doddsville, Buffett condemned the academic position that the market was efficient and that beating the S&P500 was "pure chance" by highlighting a number of students of the Graham and Dodd value investing school of thought. In addition to himself, Buffett named: Walter J. Schloss, Tom Knapp, Ed Anderson (Tweedy, Brown Inc.), Bill Ruane (Sequoia Fund, Inc.), Charles Munger, Rick Guerin (Pacific Partners, Ltd.), and Stan Perlmeter (Perlmeter Investments) as having beaten the S&P500, "year in and year out".

Public Stances

* Buffett has repeatedly criticized the financial industry for what he considers to be a proliferation of advisors who add no value but are compensated based on the volume of business transactions which they facilitate. He has pointed to the growing volume of stock trades as evidence that

an ever-greater proportion of investors' gains are going to brokers and other middlemen.

* Buffett emphasized the non-productive aspect of gold in 1998 at Harvard: "It gets dug out of the ground in Africa, or someplace. Then we melt it down, dig another hole, bury it again and pay people to stand around guarding it. It has no utility. Anyone watching from Mars would be scratching their head."

* Buffett stated that he only paid 18% of his income for 2006 ($46.9 million) in total federal taxes, while his employees paid 33% of theirs despite making far less money. Others explained this difference by saying lower tax rates for dividends and capital gains are necessary to avoid punitive double taxation, since the dividend income was already taxed at the corporate level, and the capital gains were from after-tax income that was invested. [14]

* Buffett believes that the U.S. dollar will lose value in the long run. He views the United States' expanding trade deficit as an alarming trend that will devalue the U.S. dollar and U.S. assets. As a

result it is putting a larger portion of ownership of U.S. assets in the hands of foreigners. This induced Buffett to enter the foreign currency market for the first time in 2002. However, he substantially reduced his stake in 2005 as changing interest rates increased the costs of holding currency contracts. Buffett continues to be bearish on the dollar, and says he is looking to make acquisitions of companies which derive a substantial portion of their revenues from outside the United States. Buffett invests in PetroChina Company Limited and in a rare move, posted a commentary[9] on Berkshire Hathaway's website why he will not divest from the company despite calls from some activists to do so.

* Buffett believes government should not be in the business of gambling. He believes it is a tax on ignorance. [10]

* Buffett's speeches are known for mixing serious business discussions with humor. Each year, Buffett presides over Berkshire Hathaway's annual shareholders' meeting in the Qwest Center in Omaha, Nebraska, an event drawing over 20,000 visitors from both United States and abroad,

giving it the nickname "Woodstock of Capitalism".

* Berkshire's annual reports and letters to shareholders, prepared by Buffett, frequently receive coverage by the financial media. Buffett's writings are known for containing literary quotes ranging from the Bible to Mae West, as well as Midwestern advice and numerous jokes. Various websites extol Buffett's virtues while others decry Buffett's business models or dismiss his investment advice and decisions.

* Buffett favors the inheritance tax, saying that repealing it would be like "choosing the 2020 Olympic team by picking the eldest sons of the gold-medal winners in the 2000 Olympics".[11] In 2007, Buffett testified before the Senate and urged them to preserve the estate tax so as to avoid a plutocracy. Some critics have pointed out that Buffett (and Berkshire-Hathaway) may have a personal interest in the continuation of the estate tax, since they have benefited from the estate tax in past business dealings and are also involved in developing and marketing insurance policies

which protect policy holders against future estate tax payments. [12]

* Buffett has been recognized as most responsible for FASB 123 (r), or Stock Option Expensing on the GAAP Income Statement. When asked about the subject at Berkshire Hathaway's 2004 annual meeting, he compared the United States Congress and the Securities and Exchange Commission's decision to override FASB, who wanted to consider company-issued stock-option compensation as an expense, to a bill proposed in the Indiana house for Pi to be changed from 3.14...to 3.20.

* Buffett has held fundraisers for both Hillary Clinton and Barack Obama for president. He has not indicated who he will vote for, but he has expressed that both would make "great Presidents". (http://www.cnbc.com/id/20279796)

* Buffett called the 2007-present downturn in the financial sector "poetic justice" (http://www.reuters.com/article/businessNews/idUSN0631767220080207)

Mr. Buffett was inducted into the Junior Achievement U.S. Business Hall of Fame in 1997.

Education

Woodrow Wilson High School, Washington D.C. in 1947

The Wharton School, University of Pennsylvania, 1947–1949

B.S. University of Nebraska, 1950

M.S. in Economics, Columbia University, in 1951.

Employment

1951–1954 Buffett-Falk & Co., Omaha - Investment Salesman

1954–1956 Graham-Newman Corp., New York - Securities Analyst

1956–1969 Buffett Partnership, Ltd., Omaha - General Partner

1970–Present Berkshire Hathaway Inc, Omaha - Chairman, CEO

1943: (13 years old)

* Buffett filed his first income tax return, deducting his bicycle as a work expense for $35.

1945: (15 years old)

* In his senior year of high school, Buffett and a friend spent $25 to purchase a used pinball machine, which they placed in a barber shop. Within months, they owned three machines in different locations.

1949: (19 years old)

* In 1949, he was initiated into Alpha Sigma Phi Fraternity while an undergraduate at the University of Pennsylvania. His father and uncles were also Alpha Sigma Phi brothers from the chapter at Nebraska, where Warren eventually transferred.

1950: (20 years old)

* Buffett enrolled at Columbia Business School after learning that Benjamin Graham and David Dodd, two well-known securities analysts, taught there.

1951: (21 years old)

* Buffett discovered Graham was on the Board of GEICO insurance at the time. After taking a train to Washington, D.C. on a Saturday, Buffett knocked on the door of GEICO's headquarters until a janitor allowed him in. There, he met Lorimer Davidson, the Vice President, who was to become a lasting influence on him and life-long friend.[15]

* Buffett graduated from Columbia and wanted to work on Wall Street. Buffett offered to work for Graham for free but Graham refused. He purchased a Sinclair gas station as a side investment, but that venture did not work out as well as he had hoped. Meanwhile, he worked as a stockbroker. During that time, Buffett also took a Dale Carnegie public speaking course. Using what

he learned, he felt confident enough to teach a night class at the University of Nebraska, "Investment Principles." The average age of the students he taught was more than twice his own.

1952: (22 years old)

* Buffett married Susan Thompson.

1954: (24 years old)

* Benjamin Graham offered Buffett a job at his partnership with a starting salary of $12,000 a year. Here, he worked closely with Walter Schloss.

* Susan had her second child, Howard Graham Buffett.

1956: (26 years old)

* Benjamin Graham retired and folded up his partnership.

* Buffett's personal savings are now over $140,000.

* Buffett returned home to Omaha and created Buffett Associates, Ltd., an investment partnership.

1957: (27 years old)

* Buffett had three partnerships operating the entire year.

* Buffett purchased a five-bedroom, stucco house on Farnam Street for $31,500.

* Susan was about to have her third child.

1958: (28 years old)

* Buffett had five partnerships operating the entire year.

1959: (29 years old)

* Buffett had six partnerships operating the entire year.

* Buffett was introduced to Charlie Munger.

1960: (30 years old)

* Buffett had seven partnerships operating the entire year.

* The partnerships were: Buffett Associates, Buffett Fund, Dacee, Emdee, Glenoff, Mo-Buff, and Underwood.

* Buffett asks one of his partners, a doctor, to find ten other doctors who will be willing to invest $10,000 each into his partnership. Eventually, eleven doctors agreed to invest.

1961: (31 years old)

* Buffett revealed that Sanborn Map Company accounted for 35% of the partnerships' assets.

* Buffett explained that in 1958, Sanborn sold at $45 per share when the value of the Sanborn investment portfolio was $65 per share. This meant buyers valued Sanborn at "minus $20" per share, and buyers were unwilling to pay more than

70 cents on the dollar for an investment portfolio with a map business thrown in for nothing.

* Buffett reveals that he earned a spot on the board of Sanborn.

1962: (32 years old)

* Buffett's partnerships, in January 1962, had in excess of $7,178,500 of which over $1,025,000 belonged to Buffett.

* Buffett merges all partnerships into one partnership.

* Buffett discovered a textile manufacturing firm, Berkshire Hathaway. Buffett's partnerships began purchasing shares at $7.60 per share.

1965: (35 years old)

* When Buffett's partnerships began aggressively purchasing Berkshire they paid $14.86 per share while the company had working capital (current assets minus liabilities) of $19 per share, this did

not include the value of fixed assets (factory and equipment).

* Buffett took control of Berkshire Hathaway at the board meeting and named a new President, Ken Chace, to run the company.

1966: (36 years old)

* Buffett closes the partnership to new money.

* Buffett wrote in his letter "unless it appears that circumstances have changed (under some conditions added capital would improve results) or unless new partners can bring some asset to the partnership other than simply capital, I intend to admit no additional partners to BPL."

* In a second letter, Buffett announced his first investment in a private business — Hochschild, Kohn, and Co, a privately owned Baltimore department store.

1967: (37 years old)

* Berkshire paid out its first and only dividend of 10 cents.

1969: (39 years old)

* Following his most successful year, Buffett liquidated the partnership and transferred their assets to his partners. Among the assets paid out were shares of Berkshire Hathaway.

1970: (40 years old)

* As chairman of Berkshire Hathaway, began writing his now-famous annual letters to shareholders.

1973: (43 years old)

* Berkshire began to acquire stock in the Washington Post Company. Buffett became close friends with Katharine Graham, who controlled the company and its flagship newspaper, and became a member of its board of directors.

1979: (49 years old)

* Berkshire began to acquire stock in ABC. With the stock trading at $290 per share, Buffett's net worth neared $140 million. However, he lived solely on his salary of $50,000 per year.

* Berkshire began the year trading at $775 per share, and ended at $1,310. Buffett's net worth reached $620 million, placing him on the Forbes 400 for the first time.

1988: (58 years old)

* Buffett began buying stock in Coca-Cola Company, eventually purchasing up to 7 percent of the company for $1.02 billion. It would turn out to be one of Berkshire's most lucrative investments, and one which he still holds.

1999: (69 years old)

* Buffett is named the top money manager of the 20th century in a survey by the Carson Group, ahead of Peter Lynch and John Templeton.[16]

2002: (72 years old)

* Buffett entered in $11 billion worth of forward contracts to deliver US dollars against other currencies. By April 2006, his total gain on these contracts was over $2 billion.

2004: (73 years old)

* His wife, Susan, dies.

2006: (75 years old)

* Buffett announced in June that he would give away more than 80%, or about $37 billion, of his $52 billion fortune to five foundations in annual gifts of stock, starting in July 2006. The largest contribution will go to the Bill and Melinda Gates Foundation.

2007: (76 Years old)

* In a letter to shareholders, Buffett announced that he was looking for a younger successor or perhaps successors to run his investment business.[13] Buffett had previously selected Lou

Simpson, who runs investments at Geico, to fill that role. However, Simpson is only six years younger than Buffett.

Personal Life

Buffett married Susan Thompson in 1952. They had three children, Susie, Howard, and Peter. The couple began living separately in 1977, though they remained married until her death in July 2004. His daughter Susie lives in Omaha and does charitable work through the Susan A. Buffett Foundation and is a national board member of Girls, Inc.

On his 76th birthday Buffett married his longtime companion, Astrid Menks, who had lived with him since his wife's departure. Interestingly, it was Susan Buffett who arranged for the two to meet before she left Omaha to pursue her singing career. All three were close, and holiday cards to friends were signed "Warren, Susie and Astrid" (as per Roger Lowenstein's book, Buffett: The Making of an American Capitalist). Susan Buffett briefly discussed this relationship in an interview on the Charlie Rose Show shortly before her death, in a rare glimpse into Buffett's personal life.[14]

Buffett is an avid player of the card game bridge. He has said that he spends 12 hours a week playing bridge.[15] He often plays with Bill Gates and Paul Allen.

In 2006, he sponsored a bridge match for the Buffett Cup.[16] In this event, modeled on the Ryder Cup in golf (and held immediately before it and in the same city), a team of twelve bridge players from the United States took on twelve Europeans.

Buffett's favorite place to eat is Gorat's Steak House in Omaha, where he favors the T-bone steak (cooked rare), a double order of hash browns, and Cherry Coke. According to U.S. News and World Report, he drinks about five Cherry Cokes a day. He used to drive a 2001 Lincoln Town Car[17] which he auctioned on eBay to raise money for Girls Inc.[18] He currently drives a Cadillac DTS.[19]

Warren Buffett is currently working with Christopher Webber on an animated series with DiC Entertainment chief Andy Heyward. According to information presented by Buffett at the Berkshire Hathaway annual meeting on May 6, 2006, the series will feature Buffett and Munger in roles and the series will teach children healthy financial habits for life. Cartoon drawings of Buffett and Munger were displayed throughout the events during the weekend and the special movie before the meeting began was in animation form by Heyward.

In December 2006 it was reported that Mr. Buffett does not carry a cell phone, does not have a computer at his desk, and drives his own car.[20] However, in May 2007 Richard Santulli, CEO and Chairman of NetJets, stated on the Nightly Business Report that Mr. Buffett now uses a cell phone, however he still does not use email.

Buffett's DNA report revealed that he is not related to the singer Jimmy Buffett and that his paternal ancestors hail from northern Scandinavia, while his mother's side most likely has roots in Iberia or Estonia.[21]

Further Reading

* The New Buffettology, by Mary Buffett and David Clarke (ISBN 0-684-87174-2).

* Full summary of The Essays of Warren Buffett: Lessons for Corporate America

Compilations

* Warren Buffett - A Compilation - Largest compilation on Warren Buffett on the net. This site has a complete collection of articles by Warren Buffett.

Books Recommended by Warren Buffett

* Warren Buffett - Recommendations - Here is the complete list of books by Warren Buffett recommended in his letters to shareholders.

References

1."The World's Billionaires: #2 Warren Buffet", Forbes.com, 2007-03-08. Retrieved on 2007-04-11.

2. http://www.usnews.com/usnews/biztech/articles/070729/6intro.htm

3. Helen Coster. "Carlos Slim Helu Now World's Second-Richest Man", Forbes.com, 2007-04-11. Retrieved on 2007-04-13.

4. Pallavi Gogoi. "What Warren Buffett might buy", 2007-05-08. Retrieved on 2007-05-09.

5. "Profile for BRK-A", Yahoo! Finance. Retrieved on 2008-02-01.

6. Rich Smith. "Stupid CEO Tricks", The Motley Fool, 2005-06-29. Retrieved on 2007-04-13.

7.
http://www.berkshirehathaway.com/letters/1989.html

8. "Homes Of The Billionaires", Forbes.com, 2005-03-10. Retrieved on 2007-04-13. Note that this is a changing slide show

9.
http://www.forbes.com/2005/03/10/cxbill05homeslide2.html?thisSpeed=6000000000

10. Carol J. Loomis. "Warren Buffett gives away his fortune", 2006-06-25. Retrieved on 2008-01-28.

11. "How Warren Buffet (sic) made his billions.", Rediff news, 2006-12-26. Retrieved on 2007-04-13.

12. Roger Lowenstein. Buffett: The Making of an American Capitalist. p. 58.

13. His shareholder letters are publicly available at [1].

14. Forbes 11-26-2007: 24 & 42-3.

15. Roger Lowenstein. Buffett: The Making of an American Capitalist. p. 43.

16. Business Wire. Warren Buffett and Peter Lynch Voted Top Money Managers of the Century. 1999-11-22. Retrieved on 2007-09-18.

* Lowe, Janet C. [1997] Warren Buffett Speaks : wit and wisdom from the world's greatest investor, John Wiley & Sons, Inc., pp. 164-166 (ISBN 0-471-16996-X).

* Warren Buffett Talks Business, The University of North Carolina Center for Public Television, Chapel Hill, 1995 (modified later by Buffett letter to author), p. 192.

* Warren Buffett - The Pragmatist, Esquire, June 1988, p. 159.

GNU Free Documentation License

Version 1.2, November 2002

0. PREAMBLE

The purpose of this License is to make a manual, textbook, or other functional and useful document "free" in the sense of freedom: to assure everyone the effective freedom to copy and redistribute it, with or without modifying it, either commercially or noncommercially. Secondarily, this License preserves for the author and publisher a way to get credit for their work, while not being considered responsible for modifications made by others.

This License is a kind of "copyleft", which means that derivative works of the document must themselves be free in the same sense. It complements the GNU General Public License, which is a copyleft license designed for free software.

We have designed this License in order to use it for manuals for free software, because free software needs free documentation: a free program should come with manuals providing the same freedoms that the software does. But this License is not limited to software manuals; it can be used for any textual work, regardless of subject matter or whether it is published as a printed book. We recommend this License principally for works whose purpose is instruction or reference.

1. APPLICABILITY AND DEFINITIONS

This License applies to any manual or other work, in any medium, that contains a notice placed by the copyright holder saying it can be distributed under the terms of this License. Such a notice grants a world-wide, royalty-free license, unlimited in duration, to use that work under the conditions stated herein. The "Document", below, refers to any such manual or work. Any member of the public is a licensee, and is addressed as "you". You accept the license if you copy, modify or distribute the work in a way requiring permission under copyright law.

A "Modified Version" of the Document means any work containing the Document or a portion of it, either copied verbatim, or with modifications and/or translated into another language.

A "Secondary Section" is a named appendix or a front-matter section of the Document that deals exclusively with the relationship of the publishers or authors of the Document to the Document's overall subject (or to related matters) and contains nothing that could fall directly within that overall subject. (Thus, if the Document is in part a textbook of mathematics, a Secondary Section may not explain any mathematics.) The relationship could be a matter of historical connection with the subject or with related matters, or of legal, commercial, philosophical, ethical or political position regarding them.

The "Invariant Sections" are certain Secondary Sections whose titles are designated, as being those of Invariant Sections, in the notice that says that the Document is released under this License. If a section does not fit the above definition of Secondary then it is not allowed to be designated as Invariant. The Document may contain zero Invariant Sections. If the Document does not identify any Invariant Sections then there are none.

The "Cover Texts" are certain short passages of text that are listed, as Front-Cover Texts or Back-Cover Texts, in the notice that says that the Document is released under this License. A Front-Cover Text may be at most 5 words, and a Back-Cover Text may be at most 25 words.

A "Transparent" copy of the Document means a machine-readable copy, represented in a format whose specification is available to the general public, that is suitable for revising the document straightforwardly with generic text editors or (for images composed of pixels) generic paint programs or (for drawings) some widely available drawing editor, and that is suitable for input to text formatters or for automatic translation to a variety of formats suitable for input to text formatters. A copy made in an otherwise Transparent file format whose markup, or absence of markup, has been arranged to thwart or discourage subsequent modification by readers is not Transparent. An image format is not Transparent if used for any substantial amount of text. A copy that is not "Transparent" is called "Opaque".

Examples of suitable formats for Transparent copies include plain ASCII without markup, Texinfo input format, LaTeX input format, SGML or XML using a publicly available DTD, and standard-conforming simple HTML, PostScript or PDF designed for human modification. Examples of transparent image formats include PNG, XCF and JPG. Opaque formats include proprietary formats that can be read and edited only by proprietary word processors, SGML or XML for which the DTD and/or processing tools are not generally available, and the machine-generated HTML, PostScript or PDF produced by some word processors for output purposes only.

The "Title Page" means, for a printed book, the title page itself, plus such following pages as are needed to hold, legibly, the material this License requires to appear in the title page. For works in formats which do not have any title page as such, "Title Page" means the text near the most prominent appearance of the work's title, preceding the beginning of the body of the text.

A section "Entitled XYZ" means a named subunit of the Document whose title either is precisely XYZ or contains XYZ in parentheses following text that translates XYZ in another language. (Here XYZ stands for a specific section name mentioned below, such as "Acknowledgements", "Dedications", "Endorsements", or "History".) To "Preserve the Title" of such a section when you modify the Document means that it remains a section "Entitled XYZ" according to this definition.

The Document may include Warranty Disclaimers next to the notice which states that this License applies to the Document. These Warranty Disclaimers are considered to be included by reference in this License, but only as regards disclaiming warranties: any other implication that these Warranty Disclaimers may have is void and has no effect on the meaning of this License.

2. VERBATIM COPYING

You may copy and distribute the Document in any medium, either commercially or noncommercially, provided that this License, the copyright notices, and the license notice saying this License applies to the Document are reproduced in all copies, and that you add no other conditions whatsoever to those of this License. You may not use technical measures to obstruct or control the reading or further copying of the copies you make or distribute. However, you may accept compensation in exchange for copies. If you distribute a large enough number of copies you must also follow the conditions in section 3.

You may also lend copies, under the same conditions stated above, and you may publicly display copies.

3. COPYING IN QUANTITY

If you publish printed copies (or copies in media that commonly have printed covers) of the Document, numbering more than 100, and the Document's license notice requires Cover Texts, you must enclose the copies in covers that carry, clearly and legibly, all these Cover Texts: Front-Cover Texts on the front cover, and Back-Cover Texts on the back cover. Both covers must also clearly and legibly identify you as the publisher of these copies. The front cover must present the full title with all words of the title equally prominent and visible. You may add other material on the covers in addition. Copying with changes limited to the covers, as long as they preserve the title of the Document and satisfy these conditions, can be treated as verbatim copying in other respects.

If the required texts for either cover are too voluminous to fit legibly, you should put the first ones listed (as many as fit reasonably) on the actual cover, and continue the rest onto adjacent pages.

If you publish or distribute Opaque copies of the Document numbering more than 100, you must either include a machine-readable Transparent copy along with each Opaque copy, or state in or with each Opaque copy a computer-network location from which the general network-using public has access to download using public-standard network protocols a complete Transparent copy of the Document, free of added material. If you use the latter option, you must take reasonably prudent steps, when you begin distribution of Opaque copies in quantity, to ensure that this Transparent copy will remain thus accessible at the stated location until at least one year after the last time you distribute an Opaque copy (directly or through your agents or retailers) of that edition to the public.

It is requested, but not required, that you contact the authors of the Document well before redistributing any large number of copies, to give them a chance to provide you with an updated version of the Document.

4. MODIFICATIONS

You may copy and distribute a Modified Version of the Document under the conditions of sections 2 and 3 above, provided that you release the Modified Version under precisely this License, with the Modified Version filling the role of the Document, thus licensing distribution and modification of the Modified Version to whoever possesses a copy of it. In addition, you must do these things in the Modified Version:

* A. Use in the Title Page (and on the covers, if any) a title distinct from that of the Document, and from those of previous versions (which should, if there were any, be listed in the History section of the Document). You may use the same title as a previous version if the original publisher of that version gives permission.
* B. List on the Title Page, as authors, one or more persons or entities responsible for authorship of the modifications in the Modified Version, together with at least five of the principal authors of the Document (all of its principal authors, if it has fewer than five), unless they release you from this requirement.
* C. State on the Title page the name of the publisher of the Modified Version, as the publisher.
* D. Preserve all the copyright notices of the Document.

* E. Add an appropriate copyright notice for your modifications adjacent to the other copyright notices.
* F. Include, immediately after the copyright notices, a license notice giving the public permission to use the Modified Version under the terms of this License, in the form shown in the Addendum below.
* G. Preserve in that license notice the full lists of Invariant Sections and required Cover Texts given in the Document's license notice.
* H. Include an unaltered copy of this License.
* I. Preserve the section Entitled "History", Preserve its Title, and add to it an item stating at least the title, year, new authors, and publisher of the Modified Version as given on the Title Page. If there is no section Entitled "History" in the Document, create one stating the title, year, authors, and publisher of the Document as given on its Title Page, then add an item describing the Modified Version as stated in the previous sentence.
* J. Preserve the network location, if any, given in the Document for public access to a Transparent copy of the Document, and likewise the network locations given in the Document for previous versions it was based on. These may be placed in the "History" section. You may omit a network location for a work that was published at least four years before the Document itself, or if the original publisher of the version it refers to gives permission.
* K. For any section Entitled "Acknowledgements" or "Dedications", Preserve the Title of the section, and preserve in the section all the substance and tone of each of the contributor acknowledgements and/or dedications given therein.
* L. Preserve all the Invariant Sections of the Document, unaltered in their text and in their titles. Section numbers or the equivalent are not considered part of the section titles.
* M. Delete any section Entitled "Endorsements". Such a section may not be included in the Modified Version.
* N. Do not retitle any existing section to be Entitled "Endorsements" or to conflict in title with any Invariant Section.
* O. Preserve any Warranty Disclaimers.

If the Modified Version includes new front-matter sections or appendices that qualify as Secondary Sections and contain no material copied from the Document, you may at your option designate some or all of these sections as invariant. To do this, add their titles to the list of Invariant Sections in the

Modified Version's license notice. These titles must be distinct from any other section titles.

You may add a section Entitled "Endorsements", provided it contains nothing but endorsements of your Modified Version by various parties--for example, statements of peer review or that the text has been approved by an organization as the authoritative definition of a standard.

You may add a passage of up to five words as a Front-Cover Text, and a passage of up to 25 words as a Back-Cover Text, to the end of the list of Cover Texts in the Modified Version. Only one passage of Front-Cover Text and one of Back-Cover Text may be added by (or through arrangements made by) any one entity. If the Document already includes a cover text for the same cover, previously added by you or by arrangement made by the same entity you are acting on behalf of, you may not add another; but you may replace the old one, on explicit permission from the previous publisher that added the old one.

The author(s) and publisher(s) of the Document do not by this License give permission to use their names for publicity for or to assert or imply endorsement of any Modified Version.

5. COMBINING DOCUMENTS

You may combine the Document with other documents released under this License, under the terms defined in section 4 above for modified versions, provided that you include in the combination all of the Invariant Sections of all of the original documents, unmodified, and list them all as Invariant Sections of your combined work in its license notice, and that you preserve all their Warranty Disclaimers.

The combined work need only contain one copy of this License, and multiple identical Invariant Sections may be replaced with a single copy. If there are multiple Invariant Sections with the same name but different contents, make the title of each such section unique by adding at the end of it, in parentheses, the name of the original author or publisher of that section if known, or else a unique number. Make the same adjustment to the section titles in the list of Invariant Sections in the license notice of the combined work.

In the combination, you must combine any sections Entitled "History" in the various original documents, forming one section Entitled "History"; likewise combine any sections Entitled "Acknowledgements", and any sections Entitled "Dedications". You must delete all sections Entitled "Endorsements."

6. COLLECTIONS OF DOCUMENTS

You may make a collection consisting of the Document and other documents released under this License, and replace the individual copies of this License in the various documents with a single copy that is included in the collection, provided that you follow the rules of this License for verbatim copying of each of the documents in all other respects.

You may extract a single document from such a collection, and distribute it individually under this License, provided you insert a copy of this License into the extracted document, and follow this License in all other respects regarding verbatim copying of that document.

7. AGGREGATION WITH INDEPENDENT WORKS

A compilation of the Document or its derivatives with other separate and independent documents or works, in or on a volume of a storage or distribution medium, is called an "aggregate" if the copyright resulting from the compilation is not used to limit the legal rights of the compilation's users beyond what the individual works permit. When the Document is included in an aggregate, this License does not apply to the other works in the aggregate which are not themselves derivative works of the Document.

If the Cover Text requirement of section 3 is applicable to these copies of the Document, then if the Document is less than one half of the entire aggregate, the Document's Cover Texts may be placed on covers that bracket the Document within the aggregate, or the electronic equivalent of covers if the Document is in electronic form. Otherwise they must appear on printed covers that bracket the whole aggregate.

8. TRANSLATION

Translation is considered a kind of modification, so you may distribute translations of the Document under the terms of section 4. Replacing Invariant Sections with translations requires special permission from their copyright holders, but you may include translations of some or all Invariant Sections in addition to the original versions of these Invariant Sections. You may include a translation of this License, and all the license notices in the Document, and any Warranty Disclaimers, provided that you also include the original English version of this License and the original versions of those notices and disclaimers. In case of a disagreement between the translation and the original version of this License or a notice or disclaimer, the original version will prevail.

If a section in the Document is Entitled "Acknowledgements", "Dedications", or "History", the requirement (section 4) to Preserve its Title (section 1) will typically require changing the actual title.

9. TERMINATION

You may not copy, modify, sublicense, or distribute the Document except as expressly provided for under this License. Any other attempt to copy, modify, sublicense or distribute the Document is void, and will automatically terminate your rights under this License. However, parties who have received copies, or rights, from you under this License will not have their licenses terminated so long as such parties remain in full compliance.

10. FUTURE REVISIONS OF THIS LICENSE

The Free Software Foundation may publish new, revised versions of the GNU Free Documentation License from time to time. Such new versions will be similar in spirit to the present version, but may differ in detail to address new problems or concerns. See http://www.gnu.org/copyleft/.

Each version of the License is given a distinguishing version number. If the Document specifies that a particular numbered version of this License "or any later version" applies to it, you have the option of following the terms and conditions either of that specified version or of any later version that has been published (not as a draft) by the Free Software Foundation. If the Document does not specify a version number of this License, you may choose any version ever published (not as a draft) by the Free Software Foundation.

How to use this License for your documents

To use this License in a document you have written, include a copy of the License in the document and put the following copyright and license notices just after the title page:

Copyright (c) YEAR YOUR NAME.
Permission is granted to copy, distribute and/or modify this document under the terms of the GNU Free Documentation License, Version 1.2 or any later version published by the Free Software Foundation; with no Invariant Sections, no Front-Cover Texts, and no Back-Cover Texts. A copy of the license is included in the section entitled "GNU
Free Documentation License".

If you have Invariant Sections, Front-Cover Texts and Back-Cover Texts, replace the "with...Texts." line with this:

with the Invariant Sections being LIST THEIR TITLES, with the Front-Cover Texts being LIST, and with the Back-Cover Texts being LIST.

If you have Invariant Sections without Cover Texts, or some other combination of the three, merge those two alternatives to suit the situation.

If your document contains nontrivial examples of program code, we recommend releasing these examples in parallel under your choice of free software license, such as the GNU General Public License, to permit their use in free software.

Printed in the United States
205097BV00005B/115-117/P

9 781599 861647